Walking On Neptune

ISBN : 978-1-291-48990-3

Also By Kerry Parkinson

Footsteps In The Snow
Jumping In Puddles

Thank You

As always firstly to my Nan, Betty Walker, and my Dad, Martyn Ward. I wish that you were here so that I could bore you with my 3rd book too.

To my Family. Mum, Adrian, Fiona. Teravis, Richard and Alice. You're all insane, and I love you.
All of my Cousin's, especially Mitchell Greasley for having patience with me when I am begging for yet another cover edit.

To Lindsey Craft. For Just being you, keeping me entertained, and giving me a stern talking to when I am being artistically tempered.

To Katie O'Connor, for making us laugh.

Gina Pinn, Claire O'Connor, Rosina Carr, Marina Fawson, Marcus Rose, Mark Read, Hannah Rapley, Lee Williams, Sherilyn Young and Julie Brown. My life would certainly be dull without you.

Thank you also to Natalie Martin, Shazie Clarke and the wonderful Hanson UK Street Team, for the shares of Jumping In Puddles, encouragement and support.

Contents

The Little Boat

The rocky cove was shrouded in darkness. The beating of the waves on the sand a reassuring sound. One solitary light came from the house way off, offering a security that should have been a comfort.

Out on the water, should you choose to look, was a little boat. Old and shabby and falling apart.

Once it had been new and shining bright. The name of the lover branded boldly on the side.

With pride it had been launched, that long gone summers day. When laughter filled the air and the scent of flowers assailed the senses of all around.

The joy that followed seemed endless, friendships flourished and love was made. Hours on the water of that cool still lake, where the weeping willow dipped its branches, and bid hello to the fish.

The little boat was happy, it's purpose fulfilled, when her namesake had sat at her bow. A diamond ring in her finger had shone in the sun. A promise of forever given.

The boat was not there in the chapel that day, when the two young souls were joined as one. The honeymoon was taken down by the lake. With stars shining down, there was nothing to fear.

Then came the clatter, the sound of the fight. The sound of bombs that tore through the heart. The boat was hidden, well out of reach. Her husbands gift, in the basket asleep.

Down under the roof, in that little nook she stayed, year after year, neglected. Her boards weakened with the lack of love.

The band of black on her arm, her status betrayed, the wife once more, she came. The infant no longer defenceless and small. Stood by the side, it's back to the cold wall.

Watched as it's mother moved out the boat, her hacking cough catching. Down to the water, will all of her strength, the little boat she pulled.

Wrapping her child up warm in her coat, with a small tender smile, she lifted him up. Entrusting her heart to the port.

She waded in the water. And then pushed the boat off. Waving good bye and good luck. The child made no sound as the waves lapped against the wood. The promise he made still fresh in his head.

The boat bobbed along, in water uncharted. The little boat knew it was out of its depth, the lake now a distant old friend.

The night turned to day, and then night once again, the boat held it's precious cargo with all of its might.

Then came the wind, so strong. The wood shuddered and creaked, and soon was upturned, it's bundle lost quickly, down to the deep. Battered and bruised and tossed every way. The little boat expected to break.

Into the rocks, in a little hole, the boat tried to hide it's shame. The wind still howled, and soon the stones fell, trapping the boat in a watery version of hell.

Time passed away, and the little boat knew, that it would be freed one day. When the time came, the rocks slipped away, and the safety was torn away.

Out on the water, should you choose to look, was a little boat. Old, and shabby and falling apart.

Run and Hide

I see your name appear, and I smile. How much you are starting to mean to me. Despite the way I deny that it's true.

I wonder what part you will play, in this small set of dramatics I call my life. Dare I wait and see? Or should I run and hide?

I do not trust easily, but you tear down the walls. I am trying to be open. Honest. And not scare you away.

You do not seem phased, by the way that I am. You know I am a challenge. And yet you keep coming through. You knock down my wall.

despite my reservations, and the fear held inside, my head it keeps asking, Who are you? And should I now hide?

The Fool

The words won't come out. I want to scream it at you.
Why can't you see, that how you treat me is wrong.
I guess I'm the fool, for thinking that there was
something. The hope in my heart was that ours would be
lasting.

My trust was abused. Pain still fills me now. A lump
deep down inside. I still hold my head up. I don't want to
admit I was wrong. I don't want it to be true. But it is.
You took what was offered and you tossed it aside. Until
you could use it it for your own purpose.

I put more in stock, of the bonds that were made. But I
guess I was your fool. In the game of friendship you
played.

The Solo

The small room was dark. The lightning dim. An
intimate setting. We wait for the start.
Voices hushed, with abated breath we wait, for that
magical moment when you begin.

You smile sweetly, as you look ahead. Focus not on the
people, but on the point you set.
Take out your weapon, so finely tuned.
Start your song, of summertime blues.

With hearts set trembling as each note carries, you hold
us captive. Hold still our hands as the time passes.
It is over too soon, and we all file out.
With the echo in our heads, of a night we won't forget.

Flip Side

One day you are up. So high you float away.
The next day you are crashing. Down. Hard and fast.
Either loved or unloved. The one or the least. You have
no shades of in between.
It drives me crazy to try to work out, if you are in or if
you are out. Can only be wrong or right. There is no
maybe, only yes or no. You either stop, or you go.
I see no shades of grey. No middle ground. It is never
easy to work you out.
I think you are taking one road, and then you show your
flip side, and on we go with this roller coaster life.

Cherished and Honoured

Time passes and still I hear your laugh. I look to see where you are, and there is just a gap. Feeling stronger, I tell myself that I am doing fine. I know that this is not always true, and that I miss you all of the time.
I hold on tightly to your message. I know how you want me to carry on. I fix my eyes straight forward, and try to march along.
I am told that it will get better, that the tears will cease to fall. I imprint in the memories. Vow to cherish what I had.
I hold my head up high with pride. I will honour you. I will keep your faith alive.

Distraction

Put my pen to paper. Try to block out the sound in my head of your music. You were the song I sang to, the strongest of us two. I did not feel an equal. So complete was my pride in you, and just how strong you are. So immobilised by my own fear. My words would not come out.

Then came the day when I started to grow. To stand up for myself. Now

you drive me crazy when I try to work. Try to find my own flow, when all I hear is the sound of your song.

I know it is not a battle, between your strength and mine. Once, you would have drowned me out completely. I was not strong enough to shine. My wording a hidden secret, too scared of being spoken.

Now those days have passed, and my pen has found it's place.

An individual voice, prepared to now be counted. I know that you hear me. strong and clear, and not as shy as once was. I have the courage to hold my head up high, and not to be distracted.

Games Of What If

I know I have no patience, in wanting you by my side. I want it right here this minute-but I don't want time rushing by.
I let my mind go and wander, imagining what could be. I try to forget for a moment, that what I am wanting is right now not my present.

I cast my eyes to the future, to try to see what is is ahead. Will we be old together? Would we have children, a dog and a home? Or will you be living another life? It's so easy to see that this could be where you end up. In another dimension, loving another dream. I do not want to picture you there, so I go back to the games of what if.

What if I wore a black dress, my hair in that way. Would it make a difference if I saw you on that date.
What if we just talked, what if we were young. What if I will it? Would that change what we will become?

I know these games are foolish. Everything is so uncertain, we cannot guess at what is to come. Will our dreams be our reality? Or will all of our desires change again.
Reflecting backwards cannot help us, there is no pattern to predict. We can only keep on trudging, down the path of what will be.

Strictly Come.. Strictly Go

The razzle dazzle cha cha beat, was matched only by
your dancing feet.
The glitter ball hung on that high domed roof. The sound
of the crowd was the living proof.
Of how your star was shining bright. A smile on your
face for all in sight.
You were the star of this one night show, you could win
it all with your very best go.
You took to the stage and gave a whirl, you shook your
hips, you were that girl.
With an thankful sigh, still on your feet you stood, never
hitting the ground with a massive thud.
Make your plea for the casting vote, the drum roll
thundering its final note.
The names are called, you close your eyes. You wish it
had been you, who had won that prize.

The Anniversary

Another year has come around. So quickly the day is
done. I lay and think about you now, and of those days in
the sun.

Your smile is always here with me, the way you laughed
until we cried. I hear your voice in my memory echo. To
say that you leaving wasn't goodbye.

The future looks bleak those sometimes, when I dwell on

the fact that you are gone. I long to just up and call you, I
miss how you would keep me hanging.

I know I will feel better again tomorrow. When the day
itself has passed.
It may be your anniversary. But it is one that I wish
would just pass.

Published Today!

Walking around inside your head, words upon words that you hear. Try to put them on the page, make the rhythm work.
Get it all together, and press the button go. Hope that some will like it, buy it, recognise it. To make your self worth grow.

Take to the networks, to join in the throng. Everybody is selling something. All hoping for the same. An endless twitter of the constant noise, that screams out of the page. Come and take a look at my book, I self published it today.

Turmoil

Standing at the cross roads. Not sure which way to go. The love in my heart still beats as it was. The way my head tells me to go is not your way.

The pounding internal battle rages on. I want to be with you, and yet I want you to be gone. I was so sure that it was you, that was meant to be my one. These days I love and hate you. Passion so close I cannot tell which path that I am on.

Both ways I lose, and both ways I win. Neither destination will grant me the peace of having both. Is it unfair of me to expect it? Am I destroying myself in this crazy circle I am riding?
I cannot have my cake and eat it. No matter how hard I try.

Where You Were

Should I or shouldn't I? Do I go back to that place?
Would I still look to see that smile? That face?

That you are gone, still feels so untrue. A life time of
memories to flash through my mind.

The little boat, with the blonde haired girl. My sisters
shrieks of delight. A life we knew completely gone. Why
let go, when you need to hang on?

A trip with friends, so full of promise. To that vast open
space. I can hear the thud, and know where not to step.
The best place for the fish, and the deep fried treats.

Will I see your face on these streets? Or will I hold fast,
on to the memories. All I have left.

Lying Eyes

It was your eyes that gave you away. That said all of the
words that you needed to say.

The smile on your face was all I needed to see, to tell the
importance of you and me.

So brief a hello, and yet it was enough, to show that
when it come to us, we still have that touch.

Away I walked, that night in the dark, not knowing when
I would see you again.

Now I lay awake at night, questioning my sanity and
what I saw there. Was it love that shone in your face?

Is my thinking wishful? Did I see what I was just hoping
would be. Was it my eyes that were lying to me.

Super Glue

Mending yourself is not as simple as it seems. Walk the streets and state at the rain. The drizzle of constant grey keeps reminding you that the cracks are there, and the falling water just makes them bigger. What if there was a glue, that could help you mend the cracks? To re deal the bond, and put things right?

Like precious china, you reach for the glue. Friendships to paste back the pieces of what once was. Fine lines show where the damage occurred. A fault so ragged that it becomes almost perfect. A bow of laughter places where the damage was the worst.

Build up a wall that you can't break down. Harden the outside, to protect the in. If it cannot be reached, then it cannot be touched.

If it cannot be touched, the mending cannot be undone. Let your friend hang a picture on that wall. To decorate the shell. Make it more attractive. Help hide the secrets you won't tell.

Like a dog and his wounds, seek to be alone. Alone is not enough to hold the two ends together. You need the hands of your friend to hold you fast. To help glue you back together. In the way that lasts.

Encounter With A Stranger

A hand on your arm, you turn to look. The little old lady asks if she can see your clock. You tell her the time and she smiles in thanks. You stare back at your phone. Don't give her more than a glance.

A hand on your arm, as she asks what do you think? Of the young girl on the bus, who was killed not long since? You shake your head. Not wanting to talk. This is London Town. It's not friendly at all.

A hand on your arm, her Irish lilt and blue eyes, laughs when she says on an island they should go, where they can cause no more hurt.

A hand on your arm, as she asks do you work? You answer her slowly. Not sure she is sane. Who is this woman, to talk to you again.

A hand on your arm, do you have family she says? You talk of your siblings, of the future they hope for. She smiles at you broadly. She moved here when she was young. Now almost eighty-four.

The bus, it pulls in, and you hesitate in taking your seat. Next to you she perches. Not missing a beat.

A hand on your arm, as she talks of young girls, the Germans she knew, who came the same way. To learn nursing and work here. It was different in her day.

A hand on your arm and a saucy little wink. She asks if you're courting, as you haven't got a ring.

A hand on your arm and an introduction of her name, she has been to see her son. A celebration of saint Patrick on that day.

A hand on your arm and she tells you she could dance. Her knees aren't what they were but she loved it all the same.

A hand on your arm as she tell you of the chaps. Take you home for dinner, to meet their mammy you would go.

A hand and a grin, as she tells you of the halls. The heels that they wore and of life after the war.

A hand on your arm as she asks of your dad. Hers used to send her money, to help his girl he said.

A hand and a glint as she talks of old air fares. How expensive they were, and how she used to go back there.

A hand on your arm as she asks of if you have been? To her country of birth? To the Island so green.

A hand on your arm as you tell her of what you know.

The one trip to the bay that you took not long ago.

A hand on your arm as you sit and pass the time. She tells you of her man, who is waiting at her home.

A hand on your arm and a kiss on your cheek as she bids you goodbye.

A smile on her face as she thanks the skies for her good fortune. For the chance you two should meet.

Stars

You sing of stars as I think of words. I try to heed your advice as if it would help. In time when I remember I stopped fooling myself.
Look up at the heavens and wish it was me, that I was the one you were hoping to see.
Sentiment is all that is left, of the days gone by, before this rift.
Look back now on those dying stars.
Like month old flowers in a crystal vase.
View your love and I wonder why, my tears dried up and I no longer cry. I know the reason that she is the one, we are too different. You played the game, I was too green, too mentally young. To me it was something. To you I was just for fun.
Hard to accept that there is nothing now, of the way we were, and the time we spent. Yet it is ok, I am doing just fine, I do not resent how I felt at the time.
Remember back to our friend, talking of a love you had in that when. Said she was the one but I did not believe, knew she wasn't right, that I would outlast. The confidence I had, I lost as I aged. Our story is different, we're not on the same page.
Still I look to the skies once in a while, hope that the stars are kind, as I bid you goodbye. Know it's not forever, just for a while. It is just friendship now, I seek in your smile.

The Visit

A few short days. The smile on your face. You came to stay and we made memories to cherish. A brief spell in my world, I sought to show you just the best. To make you feel special. To show how much you're missed. The laughter still sounds in my head. I love how happy you were. To see the sugar encrusted gold, at the two floors and the desert so cold.

I am going to hold you here, in my mind like this. The look in your eye as you saw the truth that was being spoken.

Those new few firsts that I was able to give you. Will they leave as big an impact on you, as your visit did to me?

Behind The Mask

What face to wear today? As if there is a choice. You know the one that it will have to be. You know that you cannot let them know the truth. The real you will be locked away, to the world you present The one you want them to see. The one with the laughter, with the smiles and the fun.
Show the world that you're happy, and that they should be happy too. To let them know the truth, now that just won't do.

You don't want to show them the fears that burn inside. The doubts in your mind, the pain in your heart. Alone you will cry, you were warned as a child. So you lock away the night, and let the light rule your day. Present that you're doing just as good as you should. That you are not lonely, alone and afraid. Keep silent all of the times that sleep is evaded. Driven away by the daemons inside. The monsters that exist deep down in your mind.

Hold fast your mask. Be sure it doesn't slip. Don't let them see that it's not your heart that they view. Keep strong the image, and their opinion of you.

The Honest Thief

The shocked silence echoed through the carriage. The man in the suit looking red in the face. In his hand was his wallet. Handed back by the other. The man who had taken it from out of it's place.

The tension was growing, with the both sides of the coin. There was a wrong, and it was done for the right.

How vulnerable are you? How open do you leave yourself? A drunken prank on a too confident man. His ego took a beating, and his point was lost.

He tried to argue it strongly, but the waste of his breath was the cost.
That it was for his own benefit, the counter argument was tossed.

The item was returned, was the point being made. It was not for keeps, that this invasion was made.

The man in the suit, saw that he wouldn't win. His enemy truly believed, it was to take on the chin.

With his dignity ruffled, he stepped off the train.
Left the honest thief to the night. Never to be heard from again.

The Star

So far across the sea you went, Pursuing young ones dreams. A smile in your heart, and hope in your eyes, you were the brightest star they'd seen. The glow was building softly. A young bug they could hold. Guide it until its beaming, and then let the brightness go.

The flash of lights, and the call of your name, whipped your head from side to side, you were still on your rise and all was beautiful. You had no need to hide. Expose it all, let them all see, all you had to give. Let them know your loves, your faith and schemes. No enemy amongst your kin.

An empty room with people in, you cannot find your face. In a hall full of mirrors you do not reflect, all that's left is your façade. The scissors snipped away. A small hole here, and a deep slash there, the fabric starts to fray.

Scream loudly out that you are still there, the young star who shone so bright. Hear the pounding of what could have been, thumping in your head.

The vultures come to claw you down. The crows drawn to your light. The harbingers sing of your demise as you start your fall from the sky, down and down until there is nothing left. No star to light the night.

Change Of Weather

Watch the sunset from my window. My gaze heading your way. I wonder what you are doing. And then I force my gaze away. I want you in my tomorrow, but I hate the way you were today. I thought we could never be broken, and then you smashed the glass to pieces.

The laughter echoed down a decade. A friendship based on respect and love.
Then the winds changed, and the rain stayed, instead of the sun.

I question if I really want to mend it, are you worth my time and effort? Am I just clinging to what once was, like it's an old and comforting habit?

Walking On Neptune

Think I will always treasure the day that we took a walk
down Neptune's arm.

Water lapping against rocks, a peaceful calm as we
gazed out at the old pier head.

Sunset casting lights of pink and purple reflecting back,
the beauty of nature and friendship.

Squeals of laughter, ice cream melting. The way I want
to keep us three. Here in this bliss.

Panic

With rain on the window, she covers her head. A groan of I don't want to resounds in from her bed.
It is so cosy and warm, relaxed and all snug. She wants just to stay here, wrapped up and content.

She checked for the time, and its twenty to nine. With an oath she panics because she is late. Throws back the duvet and shoots out of her place.

Grabbing her towel, she heads for her bath. Sinks to the floor and lets out a laugh. Her urgency faded as she heads back to bed. No work in the rain today. It's a day off instead.

www.ingramcontent.com/pod-product-compliance
Ingram Content Group UK Ltd.
Pitfield, Milton Keynes, MK11 3LW, UK
UKHW020227250726
13967UKWH00001B/239

9 781291 489903